LIGHTNING BOLT BOOKS™

Can You Tell a Coyote from a Wolf?

Buffy Silverman

Lerner Publications Company
Minneapolis

Copyright © 2012 by Lerner Publishing Group, Inc.

All rights reserved. International copyright secured. No part of this book may be reproduced, stored in a retrieval system, or transmitted in any form or by any means — electronic, mechanical, photocopying, recording, or otherwise — without the prior written permission of Lerner Publishing Group, Inc., except for the inclusion of brief quotations in an acknowledged review.

Lerner Publications Company
A division of Lerner Publishing Group, Inc.
241 First Avenue North
Minneapolis, MN 55401 U.S.A.

Website address: www.lernerbooks.com

Library of Congress Cataloging-in-Publication Data

Silverman, Buffy.
    Can you tell a coyote from a wolf? / by Buffy Silverman.
        p.   cm. — (Lightning bolt books.™ — Animal look-alikes)
    Includes index.
    ISBN 978-0-7613-6739-0 (lib. bdg. : alk. paper)
    1. Coyote — Juvenile literature. 2. Wolves — Juvenile literature. I. Title.
    QL737.C22S543 2012
    599.77'25 — dc23   2011033092

Manufactured in the United States of America
1 — CG — 12/31/11

Table of Contents

Tails Up or Tails Down?

Wolves and coyotes look a lot alike. Their ears stick up from their heads.
Their eyes stare straight ahead.

Coyotes (left) and wolves (right) look very similar. Can you spot the differences?

4

Both wolves and coyotes sniff with their noses. They both have snouts. Wolves and coyotes live in family groups. These groups are called packs.

This pack of gray wolves lives in the western United States.

But you can tell these animals apart. Look at this coyote's bushy tail. It hangs down. Coyotes run with their tails hanging like that.

Wolves run with their tails pointing straight out. They wag their tails to greet one another.

Medium or Large?

A wolf looks like a very large dog. Wolves have big heads and wide snouts. A wolf is tall and heavy.

A full-grown coyote is about as big as a medium-sized dog. Its snout is narrower than a wolf's. And its body is shorter and slimmer.

Wolves and coyotes usually hide from people. But they leave tracks in snow or mud. Wolves have big feet. Their tracks are large. And wolves have long legs. They roam far. Wolves travel up to 125 miles (200 kilometers) each night.

This photo shows how big a wolf's track is compared to a man's hand.

Coyote tracks are smaller than wolf tracks. And a coyote's legs are shorter. Coyotes do not roam as far as wolves do. A hunting coyote travels only about 2.5 miles (4 km) in a night.

Pointed or Round Ears?

Coyotes and wolves listen for soft sounds at night. Their ears help them find prey. A coyote's tall ears are pointed.

This coyote listens for prey. Prey is an animal that another animal hunts and eats.

A wolf's ears
look rounded.
They are not
as tall as a
coyote's ears.

Coyotes also listen for their pack at night. They yip and yap at one another. They howl together. Their high-pitched howls tell coyotes from other packs to stay away.

Wolves call to one
another with low-
pitched howls.
Wolf howls tell
pack members to
join a hunt.
Their howls
also tell other
packs to stay
off their
hunting grounds.

Hunting in Pairs or Packs?

Coyotes usually hunt in pairs. But some coyotes hunt alone.

Wolves often hunt with their pack. A pack usually has five to nine wolves. But some packs have more than thirty wolves. And some wolves hunt alone.

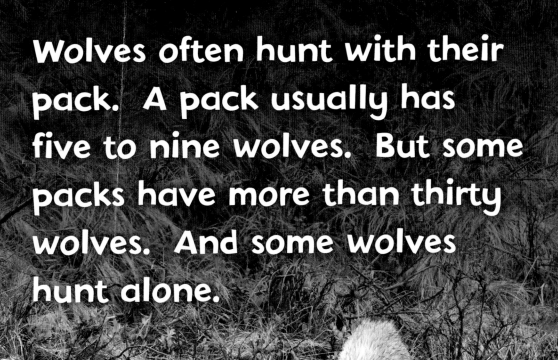

A pack of wolves eats a moose they hunted and killed.

Coyotes search for prey near their dens. A coyote sniffs for mice that tunnel under the snow.

Then it pounces.

Coyotes also hunt for rabbits, birds, snakes, and insects. They eat fruit and leaves too.

Wolf packs hunt larger animals. They chase moose, elk, bison, and reindeer. Wolves that hunt alone catch smaller animals such as beavers and rabbits.

This pack of wolves hunts an elk.

Coyotes will eat almost any food they can find. Many coyotes live near people. Some even live in cities. These coyotes often find food in trash cans.

Wolves steal food from cougars and other animals. Wolves usually stay away from people. But wolves will also eat trash if they find it.

A wolf watches for other animals as it eats a bison with a pack member.

Growing Up

Female wolves dig dens for their babies. **The babies are called pups.** A mother wolf feeds her pups milk. The pups eat bits of meat too. The whole wolf pack helps care for pups.

Mother and father coyotes often find empty woodchuck or badger burrows before the mother gives birth. A burrow is a hole or a tunnel. The mother and father dig out the burrow to make a larger den. Then the mother has her babies there. The mother and father both care for the pups.

Coyote pups peek out of their den.

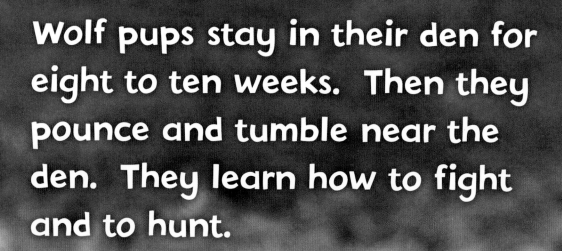

Wolf pups stay in their den for eight to ten weeks. Then they pounce and tumble near the den. They learn how to fight and to hunt.

Coyote pups grow fast. They come out of the den at three or four weeks old. Male pups leave their parents at six to nine months old. Females usually stay with their parents' pack.

A mother coyote and her pup look into their den.

At ten months old, young wolves start hunting with the pack. They travel with the pack. Many do not leave their pack until they are three years old.

These wolf pups travel with the pack.

Wolves and coyotes
howl in moonlight.

They hunt
deer and
rabbits.

Can you
tell these
look-alikes
apart?

Who Am I?

Look at the pictures below. Which ones are wolves? Which ones are coyotes?

My snout is narrow.

I have a wide snout.

I run with my tail straight out.

My tail hangs down when I run.

I look like a medium-sized dog.

I look like a very large dog.

Answers:
column 1: coyote, wolf, coyote; column 2: wolf, coyote, wolf

Fun Facts

- Coyotes and wolves sometimes have babies together. Their pups are called coywolves.

- Hunting wolves watch for circling ravens. Ravens circle over sick deer and moose. The ravens tell wolves that a meal is near. After wolves eat, ravens enjoy the leftovers.

- Coyotes sometimes hunt with badgers. Badgers dig underground. They hunt mice and other burrowing animals. Coyotes chase the prey from above. When badgers and coyotes work together, the prey cannot escape.

- Wolves once wandered throughout North America, Europe, and Asia. But people hunted them. Now coyotes live where wolves once roamed.

Glossary

burrow: a hole or tunnel that a small animal digs

den: the home or shelter of a wild animal

pack: a group of animals of the same kind that lives together

prey: an animal that is hunted and eaten by other animals

snout: the nose and jaws sticking out from the front of an animal's head

track: a footprint or other mark left by an animal as it passes through

Further Reading

Brandenburg, Jim. *Face to Face with Wolves.* Washington, DC: National Geographic, 2008.

Coyotes: National Wildlife Federation
http://www.nwf.org/Kids/Ranger-Rick/Animals/Mammals/Coyotes.aspx

Creature Features: Coyotes
http://kids.nationalgeographic.com/kids/animals/creaturefeature/coyote

Creature Features: Gray Wolves
http://kids.nationalgeographic.com/kids/animals/creaturefeature/graywolf

George, Jean Craighead. *The Wolves Are Back.* New York: Dutton Children's Books, 2008.

Krensky, Stephen. *How Coyote Stole the Summer.* Minneapolis: Millbrook Press, 2009.

Swanson, Diane. *Welcome to the World of Coyotes.* Vancouver, BC: Whitecap Books, 2010.

Index

Photo Acknowledgments

The images in this book are used with the permission of: © Outdoorsman/Dreamstime .com, pp. 1 (top), 13, 28 (top right), 31; © Kevin Gower/Dreamstime.com, p. 1 (bottom); © Gerry Lemmo, pp. 2, 4 (left), 6, 28 (middle right), 30; © Denis Pepin/Dreamstime.com , pp. 4 (right), 28 (bottom right); © Jim and Jamie Dutcher/National Geographic/Getty Images, pp. 5, 15; © T. Kitchin & V. Hurst/Photo Researchers, Inc., pp. 7, 28 (middle left); © CIheesen/Dreamstime.com, p. 8; © Konrad Wothe/Minden Pictures, p. 9; © Shattil & Rozinski/naturepl.com, p. 10; © Thomas & Pat Leeson/Photo Researchers, Inc., p. 11; © Twildlife/Dreamstime.com, pp. 12, 23, 25, 28 (top left); © Tom Walker/Visuals Unlimited, Inc., pp. 14, 28 (bottom left); © Dgareri/Dreamstime.com, p. 16; © Patrick J. Endres/Visuals Unlimited, Inc., p. 17; © James Mattil/Dreamstime.com, p. 18; © Donald M. Jones/Minden Pictures, p. 19; © NHPA/SuperStock, p. 20; © Daniel Cox/Oxford Scientific/Getty Images, pp. 21, 26; © J.-L. Klein & M.-L. Hubert/Photo Researchers, Inc., p. 22; © Jim Brandenburg/Minden Pictures, p. 24; © Flirt/SuperStock, p. 27 (top left); © Gail Shumway/Taxi/Getty Images, p. 27 (bottom right).

Front cover: © Joshua Haviv/Dreamstime.com (top); © Kevin Gower/Dreamstime.com (bottom).

Main body text set in Johann Light 30/36.